The Tiny Teapot

By Ginger England Burrows

There once was a tiny teapot that sat in the corner of a kitchen far up on top of some wooden cabinets. The teapot lived in the cobblestone home of a little old lady named Ms Pickett who lived alone Ms. Pickett had placed the teapot in that

spot using a ladder when
she moved in her house
and it had sat there for
thirty years because she
forgot all about it.
Although it did sit there
for thirty years without
her remembering it was
there, it was never
ignored.

There was the tiniest little mouse that found the tiny teapot shortly after the old lady placed it there; his name was Charlie. When Charlie found it, it was dusty a bit but he cleaned it well and then made it his home.

For years Charlie watched Ms. Pickett come and leave the kitchen and smelled her making food that let off delightful scents. He never went hungry because when she went out of the room, he would run down and help himself to a big

bowl of whatever the dish of the day was. He furnished his home over the years with items that she threw away so it was very nice and cozy.

In the kitchen there wasa big window that overlooked a beautiful pasture and lake and there was a small village not far in the distance. When Ms. Pickett went out for the day, Charlie always went to the window and watched her ride away. He could see gentlemen in top hats and ladies in long beautiful dresses with large hats and

umbrellas passing by; some strolling along and some riding in carriages. He always wished that his teapot sat on that ledge so he could have that beautiful view every day but instead, it sat in a dark corner.

Charlie took it upon himself to clean for the old lady when she left to help out since he lived there and she unknowingly fed him well. It was during that time when he would dig through her garbage pail and get new items for his home.

He always wanted to meet her and he wanted them to be friends but he was scared that she wouldn't like him because most people were scared of mice and he feared he would lose everything if she knew he was there.

Charlie always dreamt of living on that ledge and being able to speak to her as others did and enjoy the days with her company. He sometimes would stand in front of his mirror with his nice tie, top hat and cane and pretend that he was talking to

HOME
sweet
HOME

her and others with great intellect then he would dress back into his normal clothes and crawl up in his favorite chair and read parts of newspaper articles and books that he would find until he fell asleep.

One day, Ms. Pickett came scampering in the kitchen after a rain storm and slipped on water that had gathered in a small puddle and fell. Her feet both flew up in the air and her cane went flying and she couldn't get up because she could not reach her cane.

Charlie, while in his nice tie and top hat heard the commotion and slipped out of his teapot to see what was going on. He slowly peaked down from the cabinet and saw her laying on the floor; she was doing everything she could to try to get up off the loor but nothing seemed to be working; she was ust too old and frail and had not the strength get up without something to help her. Charlie wanted so bad to help but he was scared to show himself still. As she lay there, she began to cry and it was then that he knew that he had to rescue her no matter what the consequence would be! Charlie ran swiftly down the cabinet and across the floor over to the cane and as he picked it up, she saw him! She let out a small gasp, put her fingers

over her mouth briefly and said "Oh my, I've never seen a mouse like you before. I had no idea that mice could be gentlemen". Charlie pushed the cane to Ms. Pickett and said, "Here is your cane ma'am", and Ms. Pickett gasped again and said "you speak as well, well my-my"! She took the cane and pushed herself up off the floor and asked Charlie if he would sit with her and talk awhile at the table. Charlie had always dreamt of sitting at the table with her and the day had finally come and he agreed.

She made them a snack o
cheese and crackers;
Charlie just loved cheese
and they sat and talked
for a very long time.
Charlie told her that he
had lived in the tiny teapo
up in the corner at the
top of the cabinets for
almost thirty years and
she had

no idea what teapot he was talking about. She got a ladder and crawled up to see the teapot that she had forgot about so many years ago. She said looking down at Charlie, "I forgot about this tiny teapot, I've had this since I was a little girl, it was a gift from my father. I'm so glad that it has been put to good use all these years. Thank you Charlie for your help, it's so nice to have a friend again. What do you say we find a better spot for our teapot"! Just as she said that, she picked up the tiny teapot, snugged it tightly in her arm and slowly crawled back down the ladder. She then took a rag and wiped down the window ledge and placed the tiny teapot right in front of the window. Charlie let off

the biggest smile and
thanked her and told
her how he had dreamt
about this day for all
those years.
The next morning,
Charlie woke up to
sunlight in his eyes and
a big smile on his face
as he remembered
what had occurred the

night before. He got a cup of tea, put on his tie and top hat, climbed out his front door and stared at the beauty of the world with people passing by and then Ms. Pickett walked into the kitchen and Charlie tipped his hat to her and said "Top of the morning my lady, it is going to be a great day"! "And it will be every day now Charlie", said Ms. Pickett, "Because I found you"!

The End